With The Fairy Gourdmother®

Time for Gourds 8 Clock Projects

I0802340

Schiffer Publishing Ltd®

4880 Lower Valley Road • Atglen, PA • 19310

Other Schiffer Books by the Author:

Creating Gourd Birds with The Fairy Gourdmother®
978-0-7643-3735-2, $24.99

Building Gourd Birdhouses with The Fairy Gourdmother®
978-0-7643-3736-9, $24.99

Gourd Fun for Everyone
978-0-7643-3124-4, $22.99

Holiday Fun: Painting Christmas Gourds
978-0-7643-3279-1, $14.99

Library of Congress Control Number: 2012930180

Designed by RoS
Type set in MetaCondBold/Arrus BT
ISBN: 978-0-7643-3981-3

Printed in China

PUBLISHING

Schiffer Books are available at special discounts for bulk purchases for sales promotions or premiums. Special editions, including personalized covers, corporate imprints, and excerpts can be created in large quantities forw special needs. For more information contact the publisher:

Published by Schiffer Publishing Ltd.
4880 Lower Valley Road
Atglen, PA 19310

Phone: (610) 593-1777; Fax: (610) 593-2002
E-mail: Info@schifferbooks.com

For the largest selection of fine reference books on this and related subjects, please visit our web site at: **www.schifferbooks.com**

We are always looking for people to write books on new and related subjects. If you have an idea for a book, please contact us at **proposals@schifferbooks.com**

This book may be purchased from the publisher. Include $5.00 for shipping.

Please try your bookstore first.
You may write for a free catalog.

In Europe, Schiffer books are distributed by
Bushwood Books
6 Marksbury Ave.
Kew Gardens
Surrey TW9 4JF England

Phone: 44 (0) 20 8392 8585; Fax: 44 (0) 20 8392 9876
E-mail: info@bushwoodbooks.co.uk
Website: **www.bushwoodbooks.co.uk**

The gourds came from PumpkinHollow.com and Dalton Farms, 610 CR 336, Piggott, AR 72454; you can contact them through e-mail at ddalton@piggott.net or call 870-598-3568. All paints used in this book are Delta Ceramcoat and the brushes are Loew-Cornell.

Getting Ready to Paint

Every gourd is different and because they're different, each pattern in this book will require some sort of adjustment whether it's enlarging or reducing to fit your particular gourd. The best way to apply a flat pattern to a round surface is to cut the pattern tracing into pieces and then apply the individual features where needed.

Gourds are almost all water when green. To dry out to the stage where we can use them, all that water has to evaporate through the skin. In the process, they turn black and moldy. This is when first-time growers throw them away, thinking that they are ruined when actually it's just a necessary step in the process.

When they are light and the seeds rattle (usually), it's time to clean all that mold off. Soak them in the sink in a little water and bleach for a few minutes to soften the skin. They float like corks so turn them occasionally to get them wet all over. Use a plastic scrubber; most of the skin will come right off. Remove any stubborn spots with a dull paring knife. Get the gourd completely clean because anything left can flake off later and take all your hard work and paint with it. Once clean and dry, you're ready to paint.

Your "usual painting supplies" should include tracing paper, transfer paper in black and white, palette paper, a divided water tub or two water containers, Q-tips®, good grade paper towels, stylus, palette knife, short flexible ruler, kneaded eraser, sponge, and pencils, charcoal, and chalk pencils. Now, you only have to add the brushes and paints you will need and you're ready to go.

The Projects

Zebra Clock

Palette

Delta Ceramcoat

- Quaker Grey
- Trail Tan
- Black
- Burnt Umber
- White

Brushes

Loew-Cornell

- Series 7000 #6 round
- Series 7120 1/2" rake
- Series 7300 #12 flat shader
- Series 7350 10/0 liner
- Series 7520 1" wash brush

Supplies

- Blending gel
- 5" diameter bottle gourd, approx. 7" tall, 5" wide
- Plastic bag or saran wrap
- Drill with drill bit
- Wood glue
- Heavy black cord
- 4-1/2" wide wooden circle, 1" thick
- Craft saw
- 20" long 1" x 8" pine board
- 6" x 6" suede leather scrap
- Decorative beads
- Small plastic numbers
- Satin spray varnish
- Picture hanger
- Clock kit *(available from www.klockit.com)*

12
9
3
6

ZEBRA CLOCK PATTERN

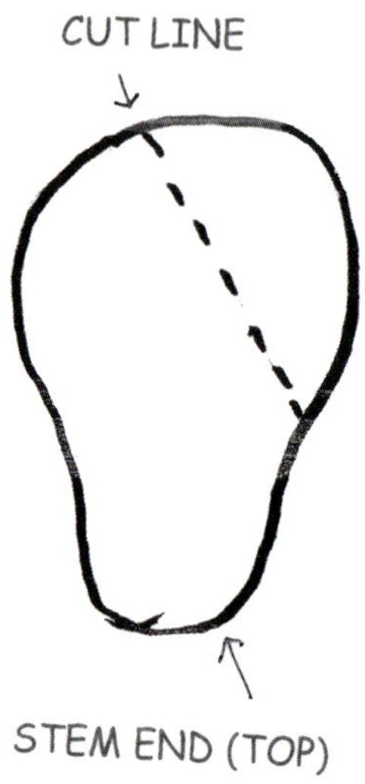

ZEBRA CLOCK PATTERN

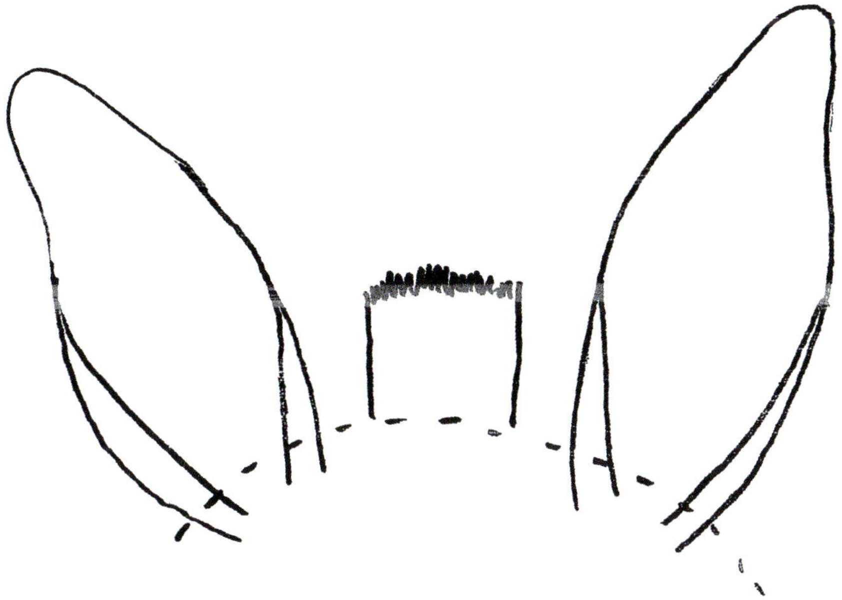

ASSEMBLING THE PIECE

Use the saw to cut the gourd on an angle as shown in the pattern. To give the gourd more glue surface, place the cut on a piece of scrap plywood and draw around it. Allowing for the thickness of the gourd, draw a second circle inside the first one. Cut the plywood on the second line. This piece should fit snugly inside the gourd. Glue in place.

On the 20" board, draw a 4-1/2" circle for the clock with the bottom of the circle 5-1/2" from the bottom of the board. Cut a hole within this circle, large enough for the clock works to pass through. Center the wooded circle on the clock over the first hole and cut a matching hole. See the clock kit for the drill size and drill a hole in the center of the 4-1/2" circle for the clock stem. Do not glue to the long board yet.

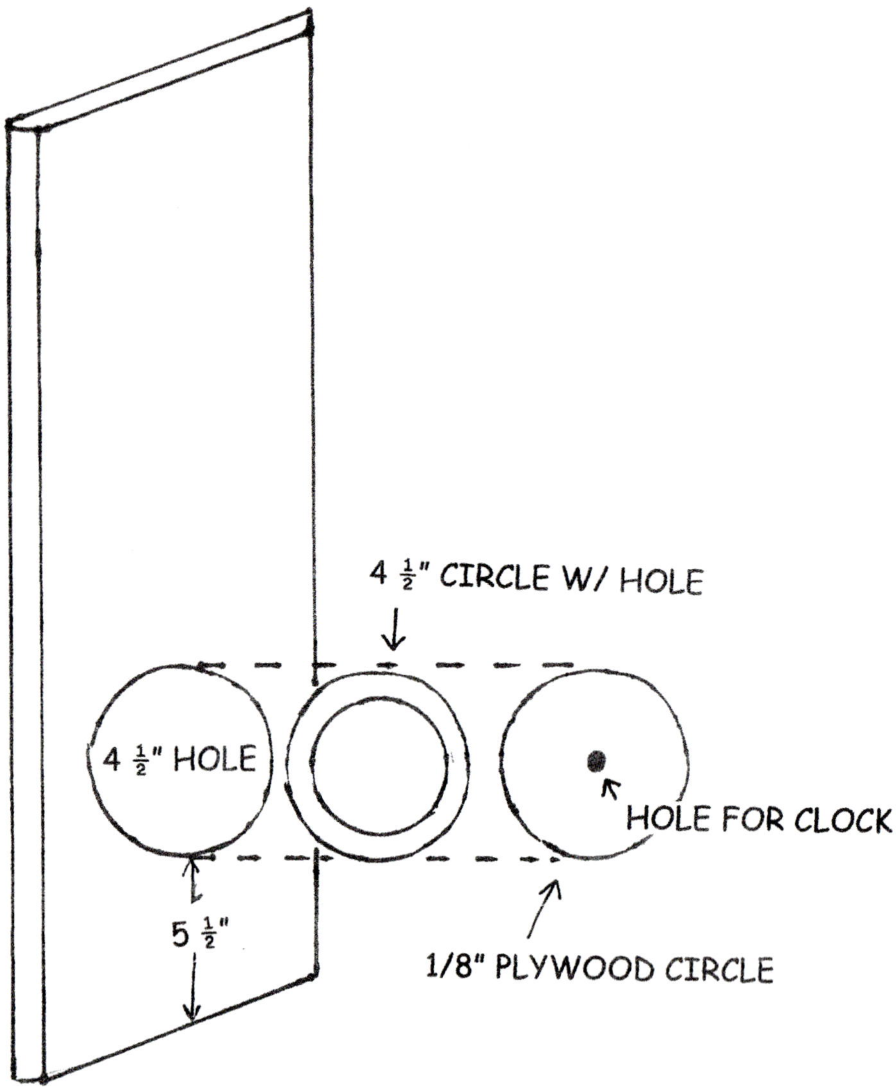

PAINTING THE PIECE

Basecoat the board Trail Tan and paint the edges Black. Apply the pattern and use the liner brush to paint the zebra stripes Burnt Umber. Use the #12 flat to float the same color around the edges of the zebras. Use the rake brush for the grass.

1

Apply blending gel to the whole surface and use the 1" wash brush to apply Burnt Umber. Work quickly.

2

Wade up a plastic shopping bag and pounce to eliminate the brush strokes and give the appearance of leather.

3

PAINTING THE PIECE

4 Use the #12 flat and White to paint the ears.

5 Float Quaker Grey inside the ears around the edges.

6 Use the liner brush and the same color to pull a few hairs inside the ears.

7 Use Black to paint stripes on the ears between the edge and the floated line.

8 Use Black and the rake brush to paint the mane. Pull a few strokes of Quaker for highlight.

9 Use the round brush and Black to paint the muzzle and the stripes on the head. Don't try to keep the stripes smooth.

10 Use Quaker Grey and the #12 flat to paint "C" strokes for the nostrils.

11 Use the #12 flat to float Quaker Grey lines around the eyes.

12 Use the same brush and White to float the eye.

PAINTING THE PIECE

13 Use the liner brush and White to place the comma stroke in the eye for highlight.

14 Use the liner brush and Black to paint the eyelashes. Use Quaker Grey where the lashes cross over the black to make them show. When dry, glue the gourd in place under his ears and finish with several light coats of spray varnish.

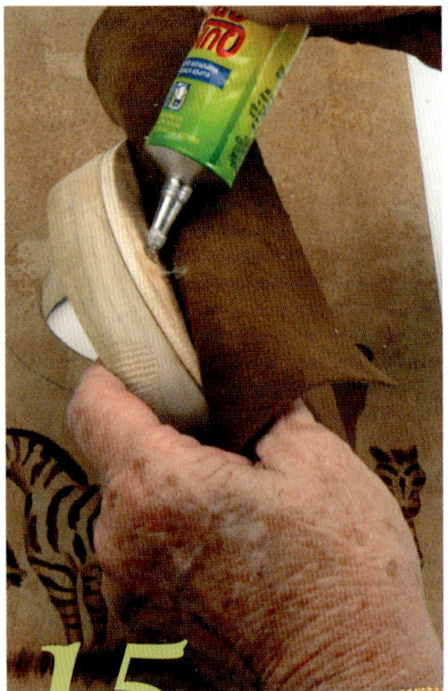

15 Glue the suede piece fuzzy side down over the wooden ring.

16 Wind several rounds of heavy black thread around the edge leaving tails to tie the beads to.

17 Trim away the excess leather and make a hole in the center for the clock stem.

18 Tie a couple of beads to each string and trim away the excess.

19 Glue the wooden ring in place.

20 After the glue has set, assemble the clock per package instructions. Attach the hanger.

21 Apply the numbers to the face of the clock, insert the battery and enjoy.

Topiary Clock

Palette

Delta Ceramcoat

- Flesh Tan
- Light Foliage
- Medium Foliage
- Dark Foliage
- Moroccan Red
- Raw Sienna

Brushes

Loew-Cornell

- Series 7300 #12 flat shader
- Series 7350 10/0 liner
- Series 7550 1" wash brush

Supplies

- 6" x 9" wooden plaque
- 2" gourd
- 2-1/2" gourd
- Wood glue
- 1-1/2" clock insert *(available from www.klockit.com)*
- 1/4" wooden dowel
- 1/2" tall half clay pot
- Spagnum moss
- Sea sponge
- Glue gun
- Craft saw
- 1/8" craft ribbon
- Satin spray varnish
- Clear shipping tape

QUARTZ

ASSEMBLING THE PIECE

Cut the gourds in half and cut a hole in the smaller one for the clock. Cut two 3/4" pieces of dowel and sand flat on one side. Cut the easel back from the plywood.

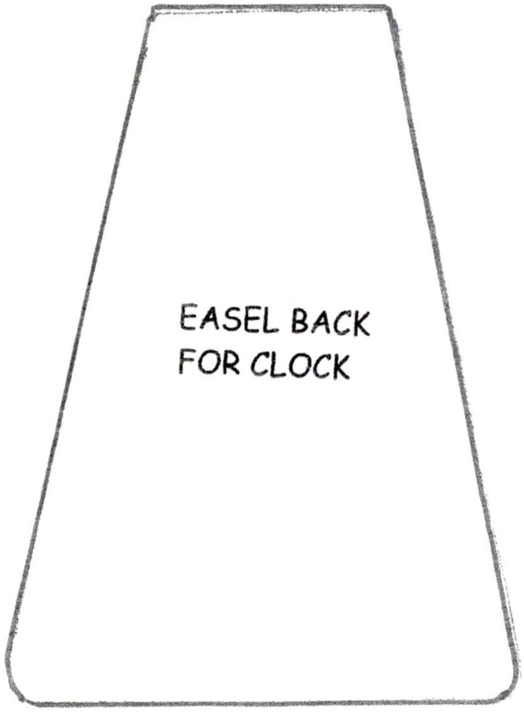

PAINTING THE PIECE

Use the wash brush and Flesh Tan to basecoat the board and easel. Use the #12 flat and Moroccan Red to paint the border.

1

Use the #12 flat to basecoat the gourds with Dark Foliage and then sponge Medium Foliage over them, leaving some of the base color showing.

2

PAINTING THE PIECE

3

Now sponge Light Foliage over the gourds most on the tops, leaving some of the previous colors showing.

4

Paint the dowels Raw Sienna. Glue the pot, dowels and gourds in place per photograph. Finish with several light coats of spray varnish. Use the glue gun to glue the moss in the pot.

Now place the clock insert.

5

Attach the easel to the back of the clock 1/4" up from the bottom using paper reinforced with the tape for a hinge. Attach the ribbon to keep the hinge from opening too far.

6

Seashore Clock

Palette

Delta Ceramcoat

- O.J.
- Azure Blue
- Black
- White
- AC Flesh
- Raw Sienna
- Tahiti Blue
- Light Foliage

Brushes

Loew-Cornell

- Series 7300 #2, 12 flat shaders
- Series 7350 10/0 liner
- Series 7550 1" wash brush

Supplies

- Small Crown of Thorns gourd
- 6" x 9" wooden plaque
- 1/4" plywood scrap
- Craft saw
- 1-1/2" clock insert *(available at www.klockit.com)*
- Wood glue
- 1/8" craft ribbon
- Blending gel
- Clear shipping tape
- Satin spray varnish

ASSEMBLING THE PIECE

Cut the gourd in half on a slight angle. Drill a hole in the board following the clock kit directions. Cut the easel back from the plywood scrap using the topiary clock pattern.

PAINTING THE PIECE

Use the wash brush and White to basecoat the board and easel back. Very lightly apply the horizon line and blending gel. Paint Tahiti Blue below the line fading down to nothing.

1

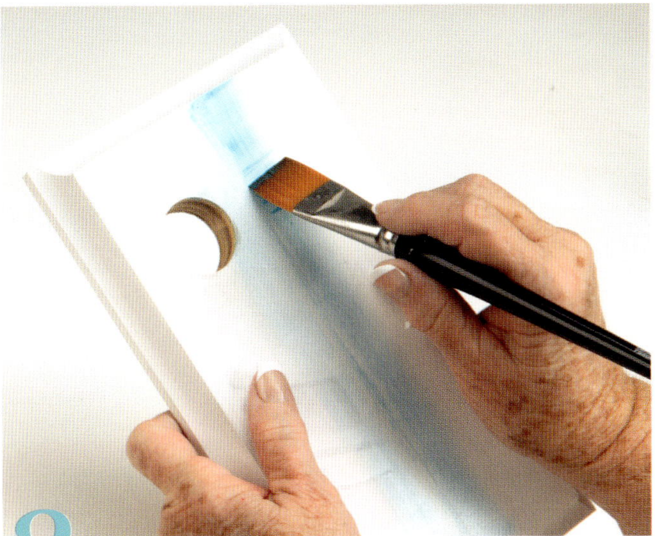

2 Apply Azure Blue above the line and fade up to nothing. Slightly blend where the two shades meet.

3 Using the chisel edge of the #12 and White, lay in the white-caps and gently blend.

4 Do the same with the clouds above the horizon.

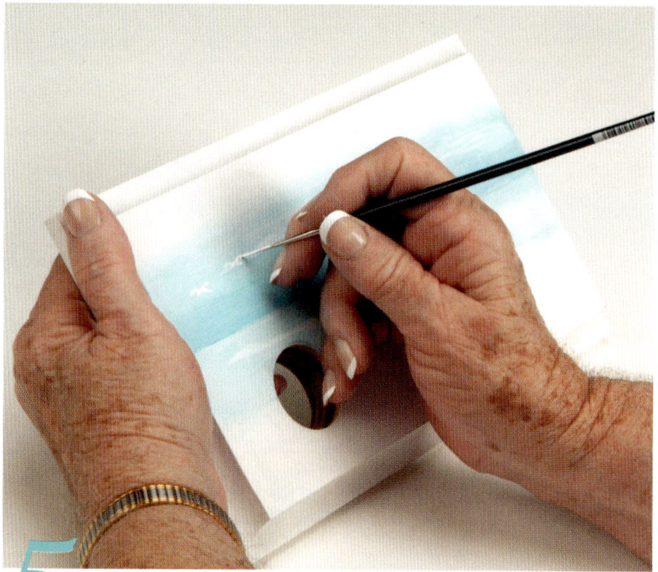

5 Use the liner brush and White to paint the two gulls.

6 Tip the wing tips with Black.

7 Use the #2 flat and Raw Sienna to paint the chair frames and umbrella handle.

PAINTING THE PIECE

8 Paint the canvas AC Flesh using the #12 flat.

9 Use the #2 flat and O.J. to paint the stripes on the chairs.

10 Basecoat the gourd White and add Light Foliage stripes. When dry, glue the gourd in place and finish with several light coats of spray varnish. Make the easel stand per directions in the Topiary clock.

11 Fit the clock insert in place.

Bear Clock

Palette

Delta Ceramcoat
- Barn Red
- Black
- White
- Spice Tan
- Raw Sienna
- Trail Tan
- Cape Cod Blue
- Golden Brown
- Nightfall
- Light Ivory
- Burnt Umber
- Empire Gold
- Opaque Red
- Territorial Beige
- Old Parchment

Brushes

Loew-Cornell
- Series 7300 #12 flat shader
- Series 7350 10/0 liner
- Series 7500 #6 filbert
- #272 round dome

Supplies

- 4-5" cannonball gourd
- Wood glue
- Picture hanger
- Satin spray varnish
- 10" x 10" piece of 1-inch Poplar
- Craft saw
- Medium grit sandpaper
- 4 bear-shaped buttons
- Wire cutters
- Clock kit *(available from www.klockit.com)*

ASSEMBLING THE PIECE

Cut the gourd in half; place one half on the corner of the wood and draw around it. Position the bear pattern by the circle and trace the outline. Cut the wood piece out and sand the edges. Drill a hole for the clock in the center of the gourd using the drill bit recommended in the clock kit. Glue the gourd to the board. Spackle any cracks.

PAINTING THE PIECE

1 Basecoat the bear Territorial Beige, the shirt Old Parchment, the gourd White and the pants Cape Cod Blue. Shade the shirt with Spice Tan.

2 Highlight the shirt using Light Ivory.

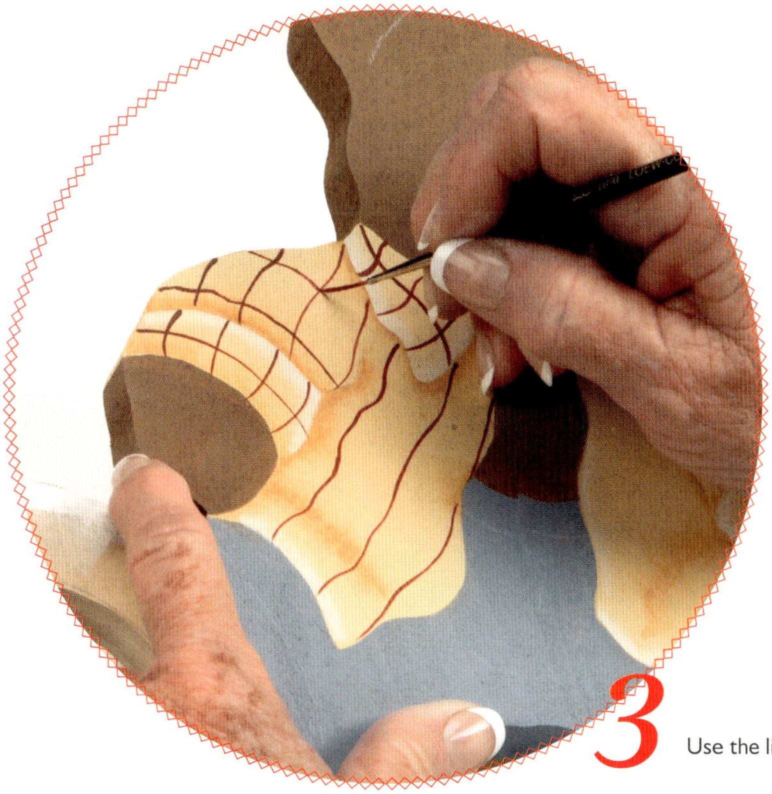

3 Use the liner brush and Barn Red to make the stripes.

PAINTING THE PIECE

4 Shade the pants with Nightfall using the #12 flat.

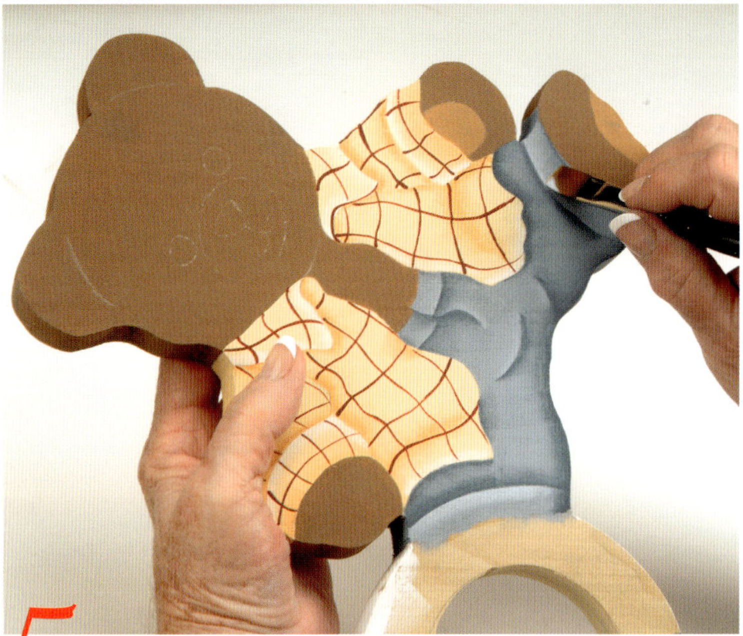

5 Highlight the pants with a mix of Cape Cod and White 1:1 using the same brush.

6 Shade the bear with Burnt Umber and stipple.

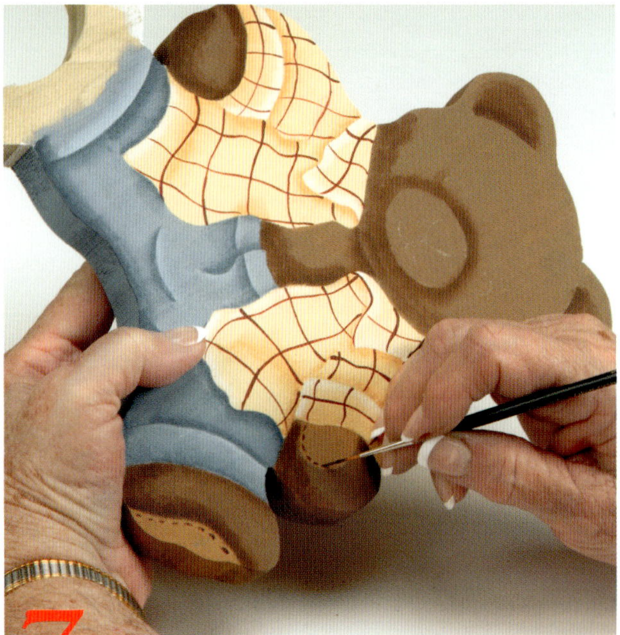

7 Use the same color and the liner brush to place the stitches on the pads.

8 Use the dome round brush and Trail to highlight the bear. Repeat with Spice Tan.

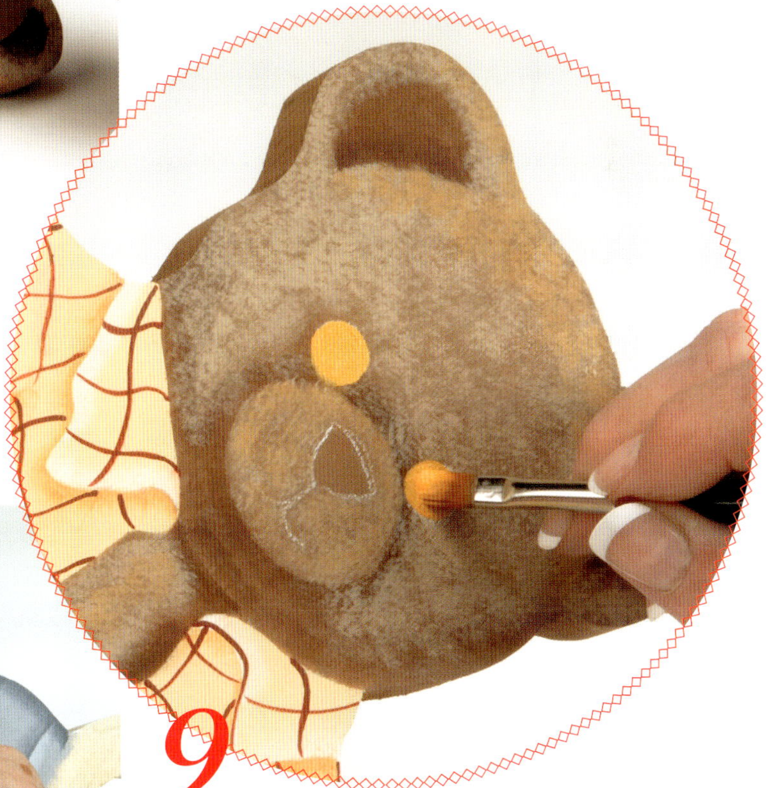

9 Use the #6 filbert to base the eyes Empire Gold.

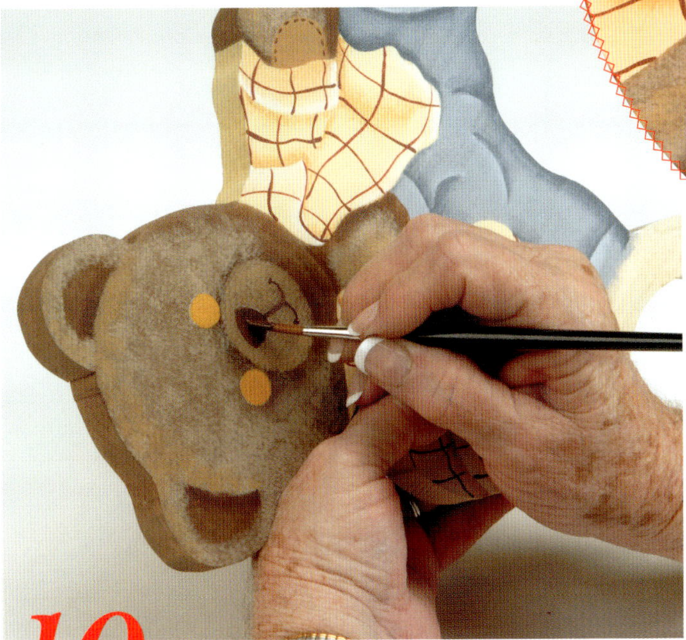

10 The nose and mouth are Burnt Umber.

PAINTING THE PIECE

11 Use the liner brush and Black to paint the pupils.

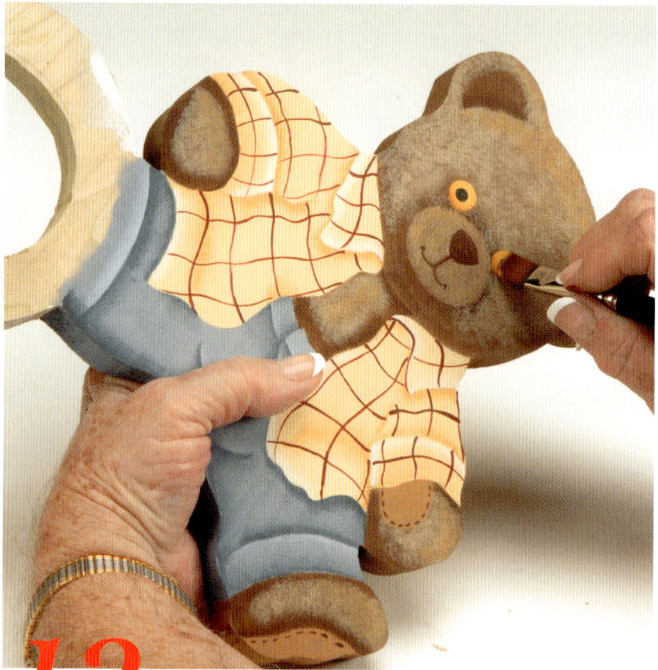

12 Shade across the bottom of the eyes using the #12 and Raw Sienna.

13 Shade across the top of the eyes using the same brush and Burnt Umber.

14 Float Burnt Umber around the outside of the eyes.

PAINTING THE PIECE

15 Use the liner brush and White to place a comma stroke in each eye.

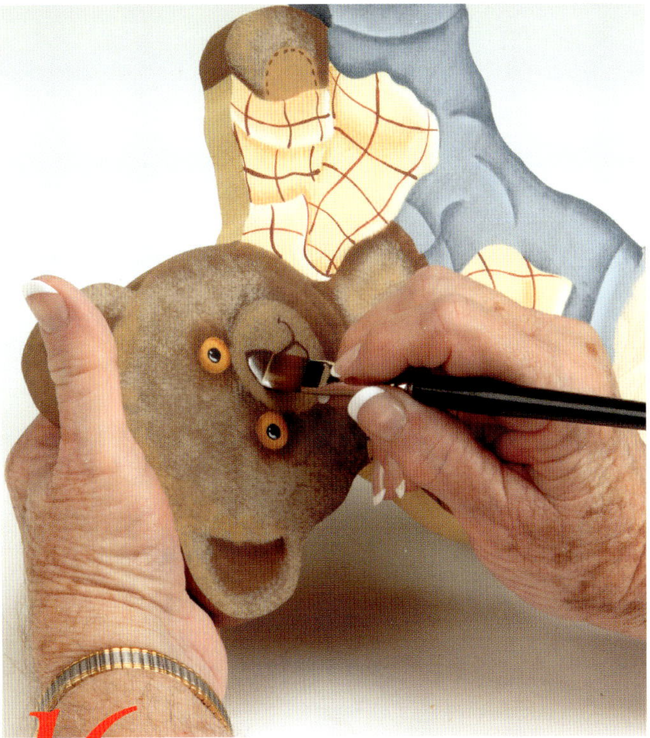

16 Use the #12 and White to float a shine across the top of the nose.

17 Divide the gourd into eight equal sections and paint every other section Opaque Red.

18 Match the markings on the gourd to the edge of the board and finish the red sections. Glue the gourd in place and finish with several light coats of spray varnish. Use the wire cutters to clip the shanks off the button backs and glue the buttons on at the 3, 6, 9, and 12 marks. Insert the clock works according to package directions. Attach the hanger.

Santa & Peppermint Clock

Palette

Delta Ceramcoat

- White
- Black
- Adobe
- Opaque Red
- Burnt Sienna
- Georgia Clay
- Wedgewood Blue
- Barn Red
- Medium Flesh
- Santa's Flesh
- Roman Stucco
- Medium Foliage
- Raw Sienna
- Autumn Brown
- Candy Bar Brown
- Perfect Highlight Red

Brushes

Loew-Cornell

- Series 7000 #6 round
- Series 7300 #12 flat shader
- Series 7350 10/0 liner
- Series 7500 #4 filbert
- Series 7520 1/2" filbert rake
- Series 7550 1" wash brush
- #272 round dome
- #275 1/2" mop

Supplies

- 6" canteen gourd
- 10" square of 1/4" plywood
- Wood glue
- 7" square of 1/4" plywood
- Blending gel
- Craft saw
- Picture hanger
- Drill with drill bit
- Fine grit sandpaper
- Gloss spray varnish
- Clock kit *(available from www.klockit.com)*

it's Christmastime
it's Christmastime
it's Christmastime
it's Christmastime

SANTA & PEPPERMINT CLOCK PATTERN

ASSEMBLING THE PIECE

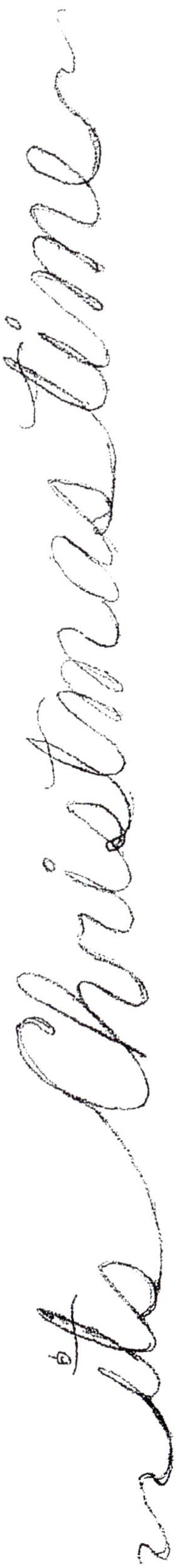

Cut the gourd in half from side to side. Place on a level surface and mark any high spots that make it uneven and then sand down these spots. Place the gourd on the 7" piece of plywood and draw around it. Allowing for the thickness of the gourd, draw a second circle inside the first. Cut and fit the plywood inside the gourd. Cut a circle out large enough for the clock to fit through. Cut a matching hole in the 10" piece once you have determined where the clock will go. Drill a hole in the center of the gourd for the clock shaft using a bit recommended in the clock kit and glue the plywood cutout inside the gourd. This gives it greater surface for the glue.

PAINTING THE PIECE

Use the 1" wash brush and White to basecoat the large plywood square and the gourd. Paint the hat, mitts, and coat Barn Red and the boots and belt Black. Base the face Medium Flesh and the hair and fur Roman Stucco. Apply pattern details and fill the eyes in solid with White.

1

Apply the pattern minus details. Float Wedgewood Blue all around the Santa to create a halo effect.

2

Shade the hat, mitts and coat with Black but keep it light.

3 Highlight the boots with Wedgewood Blue.

4 Use the liner brush and Burnt Sienna to outline the features.

5 Use a mix of Georgia Clay, Medium Flesh and Autumn Brown 2:1* to shade the face. (*denotes just a touch of that color).

6 Highlight the features with Santa's Flesh.

PAINTING THE PIECE

7

Blush the cheeks with Adobe.

8

Use the mop to soften and blend the cheeks.

9

Use the liner brush to paint the irises Wedgewood Blue.

PAINTING THE PIECE

10 Paint the pupils Black.

11 Place a White comma stroke in each eye for highlight.

12 Place a thin float of Black across the top of the eye against the upper lid.

PAINTING THE PIECE

13 Use White and the liner brush to fill in the eyebrows.

14 Use the rake brush and thinned White to fill in the beard.

15 Use White and the liner brush to fill in the moustache.

16 Use the #12 flat and thinned White to wash the beard.

17 Use the round dome to pounce White on the ball of the cap.

18 Use the rake brush and thinned White to paint the fur on the cap and coat. Leave Roman Stucco showing between strokes and around the edges for shadow.

19 Use the #12 flat and Perfect Highlight Red to highlight the coat and cap.

PAINTING THE PIECE

20 Use the #6 round and Medium Foliage to paint the holly on the cap.

21 Use the same brush and Opaque Red for the berries.

22 Shade the berries and fill in the mouth with Candy Bar Brown.

23 Use the liner brush and Medium Foliage for the lettering around the edge.

PAINTING THE PIECE

24 Divide the gourd into eight sections and paint every other one Opaque Red. Use the liner brush for the smaller stripes

25 Apply blending gel in a circle half way between the center and the edge. Tap in White and mop to soften. This makes the candy "shine."

Glue the gourd in place and finish with several light coats of spray varnish. When dry, insert the clock per package instructions. Attach the hanger to the back.

Lady's Hat Clock

Palette

Delta Ceramcoat

- Maple Sugar
- White
- Eggplant
- GP Purple
- Raw Sienna
- Denim
- Pine
- Burnt Umber
- Old Parchment
- Blue Heaven
- Dark Foliage

Brushes

Loew-Cornell

- Series 7300 #12 flat shader
- Series 7350 10/0 liner
- Series 7500 #6 filbert
- Series 7520 1/2" rake
- Series 7550 1" wash brush
- #272 round dome

Supplies

- Sea sponge
- Wood glue
- Satin spray varnish
- 6-7" cannonball gourd
- Craft saw
- Drill with drill bit
- 14" square piece of 3/8" Baltic birch plywood
- 8" plywood scrap
- Picture hanger
- Clock kit *(available from www.klockit.com)*

The Fairy Gourdmother

LADY'S HAT PATTERN

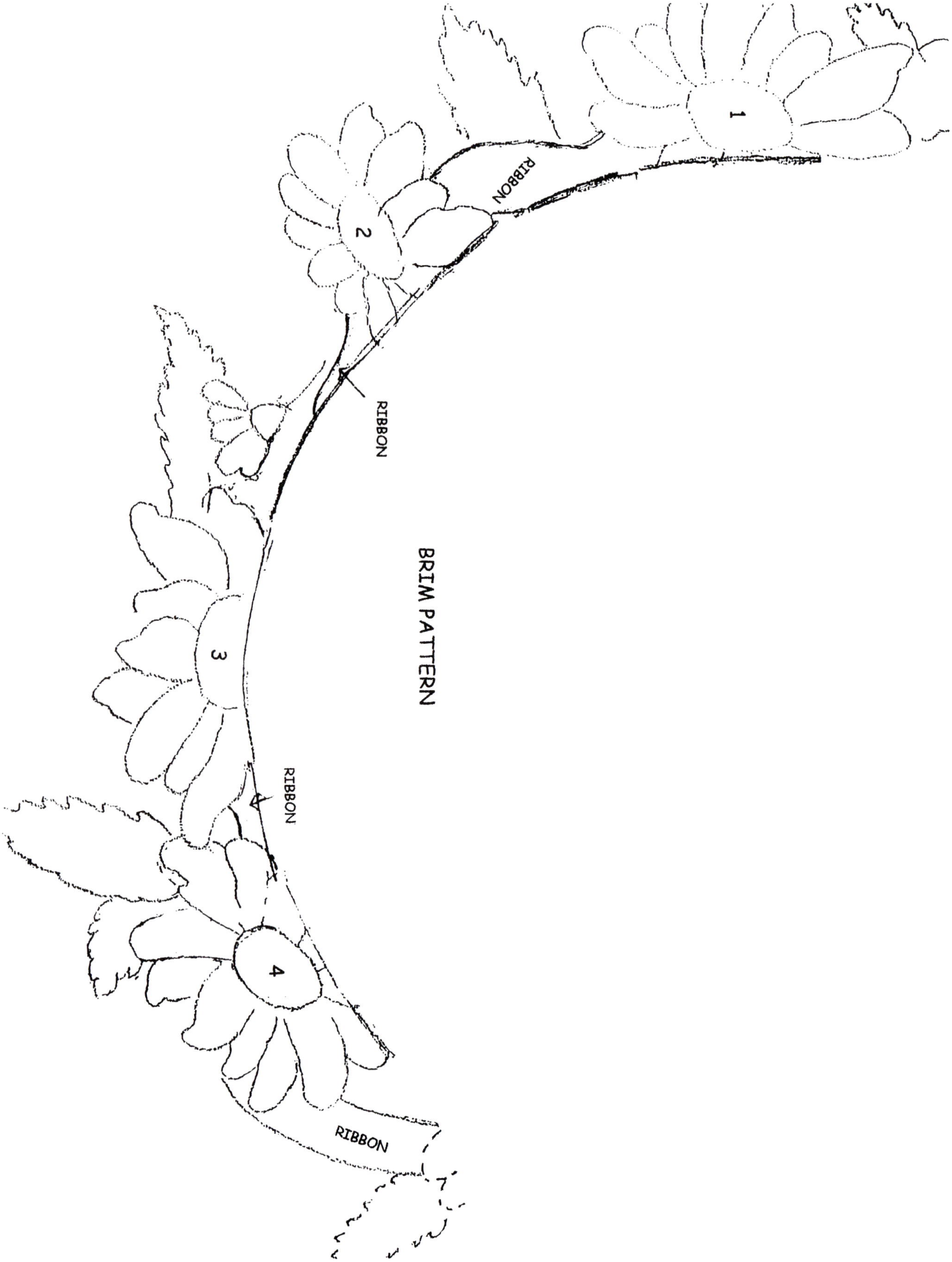

This pattern will not fit exactly due to differences in gourds. Adjust by adding or eliminating parts of the pattern. Be sure To match the crown pattern accordingly. I have numbered each Flower to aid you in matching the flower halves.

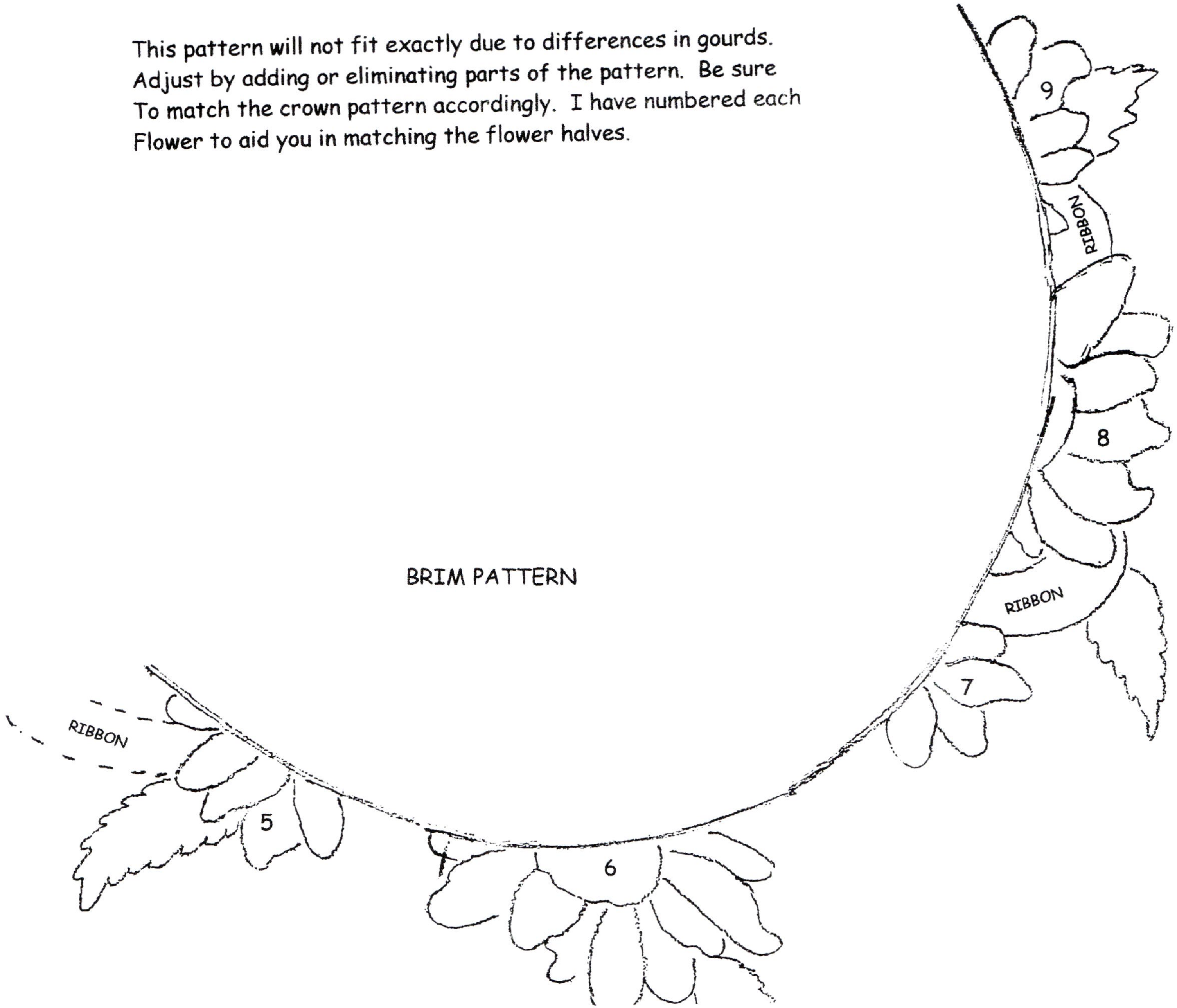

BRIM PATTERN

LADY'S HAT PATTERN

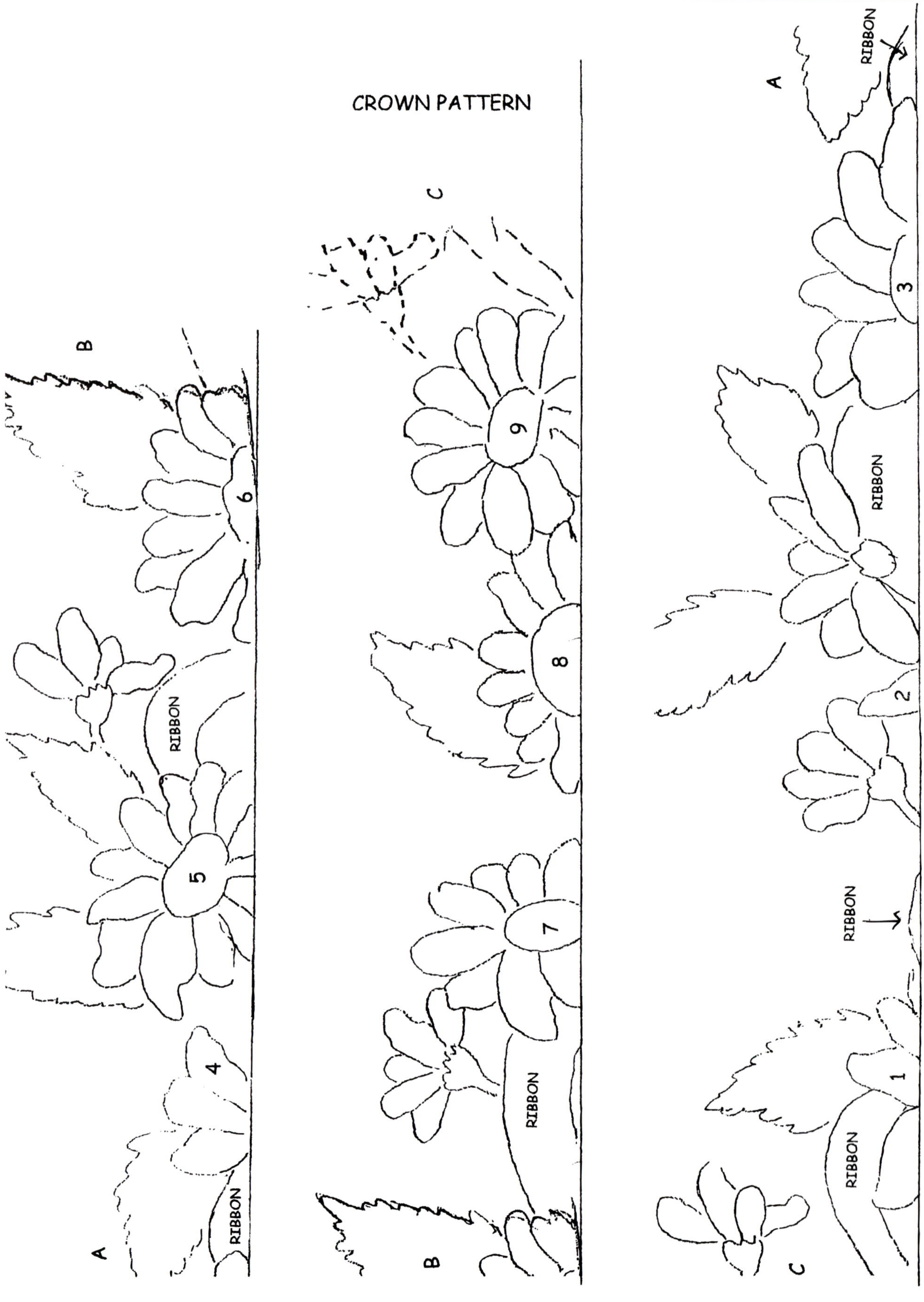

ASSEMBLING THE PIECE

Cut a 14" circle from the plywood for the brim. Cut the gourd in half from side to side. Place gourd on the wood scrap and draw around it. Allowing for the thickness of the gourd, draw a second circle inside the first and cut on this line. Fit it flush inside the gourd, but don't glue it yet. Cut a hole in both pieces of wood for the clock to fit through and a hole in the center of the gourd for the clock stem. Now glue the smaller piece inside the gourd and glue that in the center of the large circle.

PAINTING THE PIECE

Use the wash brush and Maple Sugar to basecoat the entire piece.

1 Use the #12 and Raw Sienna to float circles about 3/4" apart fading towards the edge of the hat.

2 Use the liner brush and Burnt Umber to make broken wiggly lines along the hard edge of the floated circles.

3 Use the rake brush and thinned Raw Sienna then Old Parchment to make short strokes crosswise between the circles.

4 Trace the pattern and apply the daisy centers only. This will help you in placing the filler flowers. Use the filbert brush and Old Parchment.

Use the sponge and Dark Foliage as filler leaves between the flower centers.

5

Sponge on Eggplant flowers.

6

Repeat with GP Purple more near the tops of the first flowers.

7

PAINTING THE PIECE

8

Apply the pattern and use Pine to fill in the daisy leaves and stems.

9

Paint the ribbon Blue Heaven.

Use the #12 flat to shade the ribbon with Denim.

10

Do a flip float of White on the centers of the ribbons.

11

PAINTING THE PIECE

12

Use the filbert and White to basecoat the daisy petals.

13

Shade between the petals with GP Purple, keeping it light.

14

Use the round dome brush and Raw Sienna on one side of the centers for shadow.

Pounce a little White on the opposite side for highlight.

15

Shade around the centers with GP Purple.

16

Use the liner brush and Pine to add tendrils all around. Finish with several light coats of spray varnish and insert the clock per package instructions. Add the picture hanger.

17

Hot Air Balloons Clock

Palette

Delta Ceramcoat

- Blissful Blue
- Leaf Green
- Blueberry
- Black Cherry
- Spice Brown
- Spice Tan
- Sunbright Yellow
- Poppy Orange
- Denim
- Bridgeport Grey
- Opaque Red
- White
- Straw
- Antique Gold

Brushes

Loew-Cornell

- Series 7300 #12 flat
- Series 7350 10/0 liner
- Series 7550 1" wash brush
- #275 mop

Supplies

- 2" wide dipper gourd
- 3" wide dipper gourd
- Blending gel
- 1" basket
- Picture hanger
- Wood glue
- Craft saw
- 9" x 11" wooden board
- 3-1/2" clock insert *(available from www.klockit.com)*

ASSEMBLING THE PIECE

Cut a hole in the board following the clock kit's instructions. Cut the handles off the dipper gourds and cut the balls in half lengthwise.

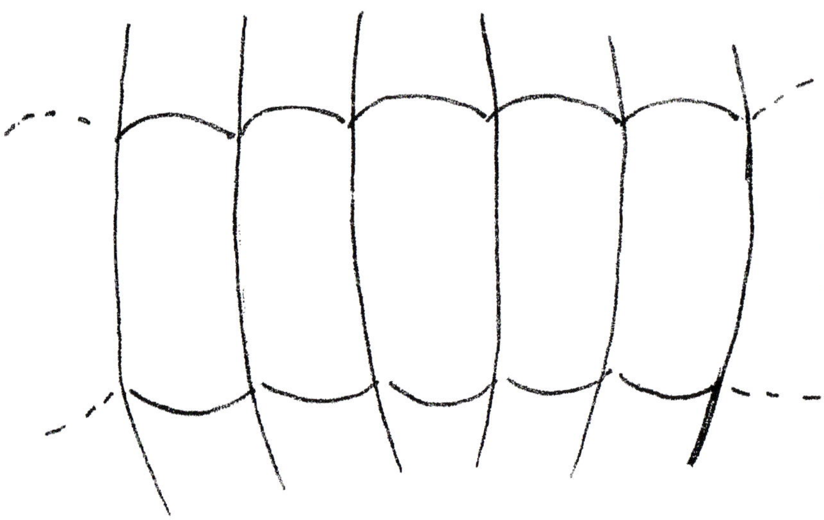

Place the smaller balloons randomly around the background per photograph.

Use the wash brush to basecoat the board Blissful Blue. Use the #12 flat to paint the edge Blueberry. Apply blending gel to the upper left corner and use the wash brush to paint Denim. Use the mop brush to blend the edges. When dry, apply the pattern and paint the smaller balloons as shown in the photograph. All the baskets are Spice Tan shaded with Spice Brown.

1 Apply blending gel across the center and the bottom of the board then use White and the chisel edge of the #12 to paint the clouds. Use the mop to soften them.

PAINTING THE PIECE

2

Base the smaller gourd White with an Opaque Red top and bottom. Shade the white portion with Bridgeport Grey.

3

Shade the red portion with Black Cherry.

4

Use the liner brush and Blueberry to paint the scalloped lines.

5 Basecoat the larger gourd Sunbright Yellow. Divide the gourd into sections using a float of Straw between them and then float lines across the gourd about one inch apart.

6 Start at the top and stair step down, using Poppy Orange,

7 Next paint Antique Gold squares in the same stair step fashion.

8 Finally paint Leaf Green squares. Repeat the pattern if you have room and wish to. Finish with several light coats of spray varnish. When dry, glue the gourds in place, glue the basket under the larger gourd, insert the clock and attach the hanger.

Cat Clock

Palette

Delta Ceramcoat
- Custard
- Charcoal
- Hippo
- Empire Gold
- Raw Sienna
- White
- Black
- Butter
- Quaker Grey
- Antique Rose

Brushes

Loew-Cornell
- Series 7120 1/2" rake
- Series 7300 #12 flat shader
- Series 7350 10/0 liner
- Series 7550 1" wash brush

Supplies

- 5" wide canteen gourd
- Craft saw
- Dipper gourd handle
- Drill with drill bit
- Wood glue
- 1" wide masking tape
- 10" square 1/2" Baltic birch plywood
- Plywood scrap
- Clock kit *(available from www.klockit.com)*

CAT PATTERN

ASSEMBLING THE PIECE

Cut the gourd in half from side to side. Divide the board into four equal parts, position the gourd in the upper left corner, and draw around it. Cut a hole in the board within the circle large enough for the clock to fit through.

Round the corners of the plywood square.

Place the gourd on a piece of scrap plywood and draw around it. Follow the directions for the Santa and Peppermint Clock for cutting and fitting the wood inside the gourd.

Place the wooden circle within the circle you drew on the larger board, mark and cut the hole. Glue the board inside flush with the edge of the gourd, but do not glue the gourd in place yet. Drill a hole in the center of the gourd for the clock stem.

Cut off three inches of the dipper handle and then cut the piece in half from top to bottom. These are the cat's ears. Cut the base to slightly curve so they will fit snugly against the other gourd. When finished they will be about 1-1/2" to 2" tall. Glue them to the canteen gourd.

PAINTING THE PIECE

GOURD CAT

Use the 1" wash brush and Custard to paint the entire board. When dry, divide into four equal parts by taping off two of the squares into stripes. See the photo. Paint the stripes Empire Gold, remove the tape immediately, and apply the pattern when dry.

1 Base the cat Quaker Grey, inside the ears Antique Rose and the eyes Butter Yellow. Use the rake brush and Hippo to make the fur. The nose and mouth are also Hippo.

2 Use the same brush and White to make the area around the nose and between the eyes lighter.

3 Use #12 and Hippo to float the mouth.

4 Use the #12 flat and Hippo to shade around edge on the nose.

5 Use the liner brush and White to make the whiskers.

6 Paint the pupils Black.

7 Use the liner brush and Custard to make radiating lines on the irises. Be sure to keep your lines straight. It's best to make a line at 3, 6, 9 o'clock and then fill in between.

8 Use the same brush and Black to fill in the corners of the eyes so that the irises look round.

9 Use the #12 flat and Black to float a line from one corner of the eye to the other, letting the line extend just a little beyond the outer edge of the eye. Keep the end of the line tapered.

10 Use the #12 and Black to float a thin line under the eyes fading down.

11 Place a White comma stroke on the nose using the liner brush.

12 Use the liner and White to place a comma stroke in each eye.

1

Paint the cat Quaker Grey and the feet, tail tip and tummy White. Use the liner brush and Charcoal to fill in the features.

2

Use the #12 and Charcoal to float around the cat's face and along the bottom edge of his back leg to separate.

Use the rake brush and Charcoal to make the darker stripes.

3

Use the liner brush and White to make the whiskers.

4

1

Basecoat the cat White. Use the #12 flat and Charcoal to shade around the edges of the cat, keeping it light.

2

Use the rake and Charcoal to make the dark spots. Keep the edges uneven.

Use the same brush and Empire Gold for the ears and lighter spots.

3

Float with Raw Sienna along the edges of the yellow spots.

4

PAINTING THE PIECE

"STRETCH"

1 Paint the feet, tummy, neck, and backside of the tail White. Use the #12 flat and Raw Sienna to shade around the yellow parts of the cat.

2 Use the same color and the rake brush to add the stripes and spots.

3 Fill the nose and eyes in and the spots where the whiskers grow with Charcoal using the liner brush.

Use the same brush and color to add the whiskers.

4

Shade between the toes with Quaker Grey.

5

PAINTING THE PIECE

"STRETCH"

6

Use the Quaker Grey to shade the back side of the tail.

7

Use the #12 flat and White to float a "c" stroke on the front edge of the eye.